LOVE WITHOUT BOUNDARIES

Mother Teresa of Calcutta

By Georges Gorrée and Jean Barbier

Translated by Paula Speakman

Our Sunday Visitor, Inc.
Huntington, Indiana 46750

LOVE WITHOUT BOUNDARIES

Mother Teresa of Calcutta

First published in English in 1974 by Veritas
Publications, Dublin, and T. Shand Alba
Publications, London

Published originally in French under the title
Amour sans Frontière by Editions du Centurion, Paris.

This paperback edition is printed by arrangement
with Veritas Publications, Dublin.

ISBN: 0-87973-679-8
Library of Congress Catalog Card Number: 75-37364

Book Design by Liam Miller
Cover Design by Eric Nesheim

1st O.S.V.[Printing, February 1976
2nd O.S.V. Printing, April 1976
3rd O.S.V. Printing, June 1976
4th O.S.V. Printing, October 1976
5th O.S.V. Printing, January 1977
6th O.S.V. Printing, September 1977
7th O.S.V. Printing, October 1978
8th O.S.V. printing, October 1980

Photos courtesy Veritas-Ciric (pp. 8,29,53),
NC News Service (pp. 21,68,77,87) and
Religious News Service (pp. 13,36,45,60).

Published, printed and bound in the U.S.A. by
Our Sunday Visitor, Inc.
200 Noll Plaza
Huntington, Indiana 46750

679

Contents

Agnes Gonxha Bojaxhiu

CORPORATION OF CALCUTTA
NIRMAL HRIDAY
HOME FOR DYING DESTITUTES

কলিকাতা পৌর প্রতিষ্ঠান

নির্মল হৃদয়

মুমূর্ষু নিরাশ্রয়দের আশ্রয়স্থল

On the front of a house in Calcutta is a plaque
with the inscription:

Corporation of Calcutta

Nirmal Hriday

Home for Dying Destitutes

Inside, in the subdued light from the coloured
windows, are three rows of people lying on camp
beds. "These men and women," a nun explains,
"are all either unconscious or semi-conscious,
homeless people the overcrowded hospitals cannot
accommodate. As soon as we find them dying on
the streets we 'phone for an ambulance and bring
them here. Sometimes those who are still conscious
refuse to come. Some come of their own accord,
to die in peace. Since the home opened more than·
26,000 people have been admitted. Half of these
died within a few hours. Others have survived;
but for what?"

The house has two rooms, one for men, one for
women, each room having 72 beds. The nun and
her visitor move from one to the other, lifting the
covers from the faces and driving away flies which
stick to the transparent skin. Are they dead? Or is
it possible they're still alive? The nun says they

have never known anything but the streets and the depths of degradation. "They have lived like animals," says a voice, "but here they die like saints."

It is Mother Teresa, the woman who amazes the world. She wears a white cotton sari with a wide blue border, a piece of which forms an Indian-style coif. A crucifix is discreetly placed on her left shoulder. Her face is neither beautiful nor slender, but rather that of a solid peasant: a strong nose, large nostrils, with a fine down on her upper lip. Her eyes are bright, almost luminous, and not without malice; her smile is tender and welcoming. What sort of woman is she, to have come so far to fight against hunger and death?

The daughter of an Albanian chemist, Agnes Gonxha Bojaxhiu was born on the 27th August 1910 in Skopje, Yugoslavia. As a young girl she was pious and well-behaved, and would have made someone a good wife, if at the age of twelve she had not become aware of another calling. Six years later some Jesuit fathers told her about the Sisters of Our Lady of Loretto in Calcutta. And that was it! She was accepted as a postulant at the Mother-house of the order at Rathfarnham, Dublin; and at the age of eighteen was on her way to Calcutta. Nine years went by, at the end of which she made her three vows of poverty, chastity and obedience. She then taught for several years in the school attached to the convent.

But during this time something troubled her. At first it was only minor, but each year it grew,

challenging the comfort and order of the class-
rooms where she had been endowing with culture
and the norms of a good education the docile
daughters of the rich.

It was the voice of poverty ringing in her ears
from beyond the cloister; hands were stretching
out in their thousands from the street,
asking something completely different of her;
the groans of the destitute, dying in squalor on
the pavements of this nightmare city, were chilling
her heart.

The Call of Poverty

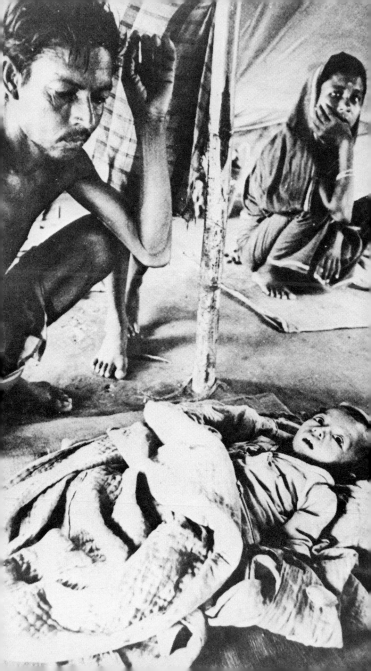

In Calcutta alone there are more than 400,000
homeless. In the railway stations thousands of
men, women and children sleep among parcels of
laundry on the cement floor of the hallway. Outside — a swarming mass of humanity, which looks
as if it has come from some enormous, ripped-
open anthill. Amid the squalor, four ragged little
angels are playing. A squatting woman picks up a
child and opens her sari to expose a shrivelled
breast. The baby seizes it greedily, then slumps on
the cobbles. The mother dresses herself. She is
expecting her fifth baby.

Vultures hover all around, while apple-green
birds with long tapering beaks hop about among
the passengers' suitcases.

The bridge over the Hoogly River screens a
scene of horror: beggars and cripples ask for
alms; against an iron girder a man is dying, lying
on his side with his mouth open, letting a pinkish
dribble escape with an intermittent whistling
sound. A few yards away, a mob has gathered
around a strange form, a man who seems to be
all head. His head is of normal size. His arms and
legs are broom-sticks. A blind man slides along

on his back, his body the grey colour of the path. Only the sores on his shoulder-blades are red.

Where do these poor creatures live? Down there, under the mud walls, they have a room seven or eight metres square, per family; it has no water or electricity, yet it costs twenty rupees a month; inside are a few beds and mats made of banana leaves. In the evening thousands of stoves will be lit to cook the meagre ration (a hundred rupees a month doesn't buy much). And what do they use for fuel? Cakes of cow-dung moulded by the women: three for a centime.

The food ration in calories is the poorest in the world. Pangs of hunger cripple the unfortunate people, even when they are asleep; their stomachs complain insistently and they feel a gnawing deep inside them, as if a wild beast were attacking their vital organs.

The pain dulls but never goes away: every time they think of food, an awful sickness comes over them. They try not to think about it, but the hunger is always there. After this stage there is a deep void; their strength leaves them; they can no longer get up, and lack even the strength to swallow a mouthful of water.

That is India's first problem. Unrest, continuous strikes, the weakening climate, lack of hygiene all contribute to make these human problems even more dramatic, and to cut down the rations even further: 160 grams of rice a day only keeps their stabbing hunger alive. And in order to get their rations at the corner stall, they must queue for hours, sometimes only to be told that there is none left. Then they have to borrow from the money-lenders to buy things on the black market, where a kilo of rice costs three times its official price. The turbaned money-lenders have no scruples, and in a single deal they take in a third of the monthly wage. In December 1965, hunger had reached such a pitch that the governor of Orissa stated in parliament: "The farmers in my state are obliged to sell not only their goods, but their children."

Along with rice, the staple diet is the famous Bulgur, about which one of the nuns said, somewhat humorously: "If I haven't lost an ounce of weight since my arrival, it is undoubtedly due to American Bulgur, a crude wheat which when cooked resembles duck-mash . . . By way of gratitude to the American people, I have proposed that the next postulant be called 'Sister Bulgur' , because not only do we eat it, but the packing in which it comes is used to make shirts, bedspreads, and curtains. . . It is wonderful, and even more so because the directions for the use of this Bulgur are written in eight languages.

But even the amusing Bulgur doesn't prevent India from being a country of such misery that the Ford Foundation report says: "Nowhere else in the world have we seen degradation on such a scale."

The causes seem to be multiple: first of all, these poor creatures are the victims of a social system which makes those who do not fit into the four principal classes, social outcasts. But Gandhi preferred to call them the "Sons of God".

There are four main classes: the Brahmans, the warriors, the traders, and the farmers. Any man born outside these strictly defined classes is an outcast, a nobody — and there are sixty thousand of those.

The Hindu is by nature resigned to his fate, that is to say resigned to the class into which he was born. The classes mark the stages of crossing the *samsara*, that is, to successive existences. A person is reborn to a higher or lower class according to the *karma*, more or less accumulated during previous existences.

The brahman is esteemed because he is rich and powerful, and because he has a good *karma;* but if he is not virtuous he will become a person to be avoided. So social injustice is accepted as a consequence of former actions, and with faith in a compensatory transmigration. It is therefore considered useless to reform the social order.

As a result, the economic situation never ceases to deteriorate. In the rural areas many peasants, who have no land-rights in the forest and mountain regions they have cultivated, are threatened with expulsion. There is no work for those who are looking for it, and there are no grants, unemployment benefits, or social security. How do you find work for everyone in an overpopulated country, even by increasing personnel? Where one man would be sufficient to complete a task, you'll find four or five doing it at different stages.

In the stations, the undernourished porters put down their burdens every three metres, where they pay a forfeit to the head-porter out of gratitude for being allowed to work. The head-porter then discharges a higher fee to another official and so on to the centre of Administration. Hotel room service is divided between six employees, from the turbaned boy who never does anything, to the bathroom cleaner and the filthily dressed outcast who cleans the toilets.

The black-bearded sikh taxi driver is accompanied by two men whose job it is to open and close the doors. In this way several people are maintained on one salary, which would scarcely be sufficient to feed one of them.

Many people are trying to correct this state of affairs; and even the government is trying to remedy it, but they are all meeting with large obstacles: this extreme division of labour is greatly aggravated by the social system which forbids a person to engage in an activity foreign to his hereditary profession; and by the tradition of family unity which leaves a salaried person with fifteen idle people to support. This distribution of labour according to birth goes on even among the outcasts, where strict divisions separate the butcher, the curer and the cobbler from their brothers, because they have been soiled by contact with the hide of sacred cows.

The Indians need a lot of imagination to survive, and plenty of ingenuity to earn a few rupees: some of the women carry buckets of coal; others carry bricks on their heads up to the twenty-fifth storey of houses under construction for two rupees a day, which is about 12 NP for eight hours' work.

But in spite of their misery, the people have retained their dignity. Many of them help one another, and their tactfulness is extraordinary. A worker will undertake a four-hour walk to his job to save the thirty-two centime fare for someone poorer than himself. Another will give twenty rupees of his salary to pay the hospitalisation costs of a destitute widow and mother. Some of them are gentle to a degree which is almost painful to behold among such an oppressed people, incapable of resentment, envy or ill-feeling towards the people of another race so clearly more privileged than themselves. If you go into their homes, they offer you bitter coffee, without sugar, in the tin pot in which they have made the curry. You can walk alone, well-dressed, in the poorest quarters without ever feeling a reprobatory glance, which would indeed be quite justified. And in the evening the bright lights from the petrol wells overshadow the dirty laneways, making the city look like a milky way, lighting up the high-class hotels, and seeming to smooth over class difference. And yet the contrast between the classes is so pronounced that a little nun in the Loretto convent is frightened by the imbalance of it. "Something must be done; I must do something!"

Time to Make the Break

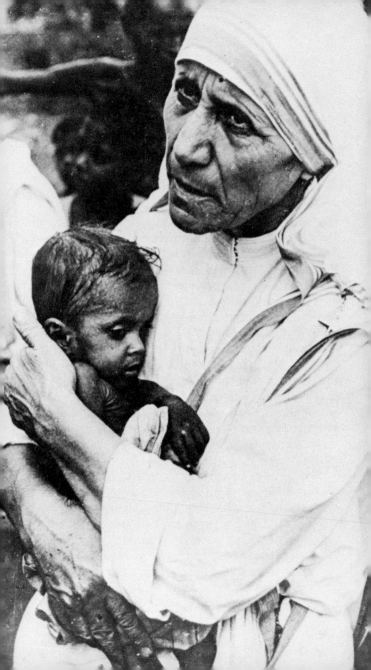

One summer, Sister Teresa went by train to
Darjeeling to make her annual retreat. It was
September 10th, 1946, and she slept little during
the overnight journey. There were all kinds of
pictures running through her mind: she was
hurrying along the stinking paths of the slums
and the tottering stairways of buildings, coming
upon dwellings unfit for dogs. She saw a little
eight-year-old girl dying of hunger; abandoned
children like living skeletons; and in the dustbins,
the drains, under the bus-seats there were living
fetuses, given to the dogs to eat. A little boy
whose mother had tried to kill him still had the
strangle marks on his neck. Could she be dreaming?
Sister Teresa was greatly disturbed by the strange
vision.

   She could not accustom herself to the idea of
all this suffering. Yet she was protected from it,
enclosed in a comfortable bourgeois school. In the
railway carriage the rhythmic hammering of the
wheels repeated in her ears: "I must do something."
It was a message too clear to be misunderstood.
She must leave the convent and devote herself to
these poor people.

When she understood at last what God wanted of her it seemed too much. She murmured incredulously: "Lord, is this possible? Am I, a poor little nun threatened by tuberculosis, to leave my convent, my community, and the life I'm used to? I could never survive!"

Nevertheless, her retreat only strengthened her resolution. She decided to leave. When she returned to Calcutta she asked the archbishop, Monsignor Ferdinand Périer, for permission to leave the order and devote herself exclusively to the poor. The prelate's reply was conclusive, and negative. Later she would explain: "There was nothing else he could say. An archbishop can't give permission to found a new order to the first nun who comes along, saying God has asked it of her."

But time is the surest criterion; it either discourages or stimulates: a year later Teresa reiterated her request, and now the archbishop advised her to seek the permission, first, of the motherhouse of the Order. Mother Gertrude, Mother-General of the congregation, a discerning woman, recognised the voice of God in Teresa's letter. "If God is calling you, I give you my permission with all my heart. I want you to know that we love you, and if you ever want to come back to us, there will always be a place for you."

Teresa's unusual request "to live alone outside the cloister among the poor of Calcutta, with God alone as protector and guide", was sent to Rome. On April 12th, 1948, Pius XII gave Teresa per-

mission to leave Our Lady of Loretto Convent,
while remaining a nun under the jurisdiction of
the Archbishop of Calcutta. She was now free to
enter the world of the poor.

For four rupees she bought a white cotton sari
with a blue border and put a small cross on the
shoulder. After a three-month course with the
Medical Sisters at Patna she returned to Calcutta,
where she sought out the most miserable slums in
Tiljala and Motijhil.

Going from one hut to the next, she set to work
with soap and water. The Indian women watched
what she was doing. Smiling all the time, she washed,
fed and cared for the children of those hungry
men and women, who were wondering what could
be their purpose in life.

After three days she started an open-air school:
twenty-three pupils attended the first day, forty-
one the second. "We used the ground for a black-
board, and I used to begin by washing the children."
She smiled at this memory but the smile quickly
faded, because even though contact with children
made her happy, the daily sight of the sick and
dying filled her with awe at the intensity of the
task before her. "It's like being shipwrecked,"
she wrote, "in an ocean of misery and despair.
God wants me as an uncloistered nun, clothed in
the poverty of the Cross. But today I have learned
something . . . The most destitute need a roof over
their heads, so I set out to look for one and walked
and walked until I could go no further. Then I
understood a bit better how exhausted the really
poor must get, walking around in search of food

or medicine; it was then that the thought of the comfortable life of the Loretto convent really tempted me. My God, because of my free choice and for love of you alone, I am going to stay here and do what your will demands of me."

And she continued her never-ending journey through the brimming river of streets, which carried her along like a piece of straw. Out in the open, before she even went into the alleys of George Town, she was literally assailed by a count-less army of beggars who followed her with the monotonous chant: "Mê. . . Mê . . ." She was cornered by starving urchins chanting a horrible litany: "No father. . . no mother . . . no brother. Foreigner, give money!" People with one eye, or one arm, lepers or venereals, nameless faces on ill-formed bodies, creatures whose sex or age it was impossible to determine, all pointed their fingers to their mouths to show that they were hungry. Some were naked and unable to stand up, and they followed her on all fours.

But these were not the people Mother Teresa was seeking, for they were still capable of getting around. She moved towards those stretched out on the pavements of whom it was impossible to say whether they were alive or dead.

"I took the first woman I saw off the street. She was half eaten by rats and ants. I brought her to the hospital, but there was nothing they could do for her, and in fact they only kept her because I refused to go away until they admitted her." Then she found an old lady who had been thrown out among the litter. Mother Teresa freed her, and the old lady saw her feeble frame bending over her, clad in a rough sari, her face already thin with brown circles under her eyes. Weeping, the old lady said: "It was my own son who did this to me."

The next day Mother Teresa set off again, but her legs refused to carry her and her whole body ached. She went home worn out, with the same thought running through her mind: "Are you really sure this is what God wants of you? Remember Loretto Convent with the nuns, the peace of a regular life which offers security and protection? Must you do all this?"

She had only to say the word and she could take her place again in the community instead of coming back day after day to the filthy laneways, the skeletal faces, the dampness of feverish bodies, the beds crawling with vermin, the stench of the dying. The temptation was strong as she crossed Calcutta in the evening after her day's work. "No," she repeated, "I will not go back. My true community is the poor — their security is my security, their health is my health. My home is among the poor, and not only the poor, but the poorest of them: the people no one will go near because they are filthy and suffering from contagious diseases, full of germs and vermin-infested — the people who can't go to church because they can't go out naked — the people who can no longer eat because they haven't the strength — the people who lie down in the street, knowing they are going to die, while others look away and pass them by — the people who no longer cry because their tears have run dry! The Lord wants me exactly where I am — he will provide the answers."

"I have noticed," says don Giovanni Zempetti, "that in the life of every 'founder' there is a given moment — and it is always a moment of decision — when the shadow of a providential figure appears on the scene, gifted with means and possibilities, and manages to resolve material problems which seemed insoluble."

In this case the figure was Michel Gomez, a state administration official, who put a room on the top floor of a Creek Lane house at Mother Teresa's disposal. At the same time came help and support from many people, especially teachers, students, the mothers of families. The Hindus were overwhelmed by their charity.

Around the Shanty-Towns

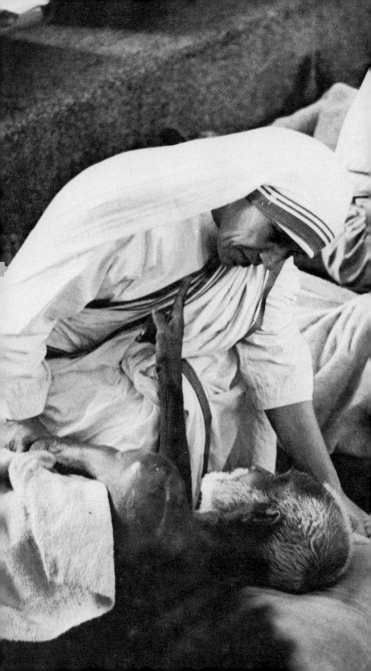

On meeting Mother Teresa a Protestant lady said
to her: "For nine years I have been praying that
God would send someone to these people, and
here you are! May I come and listen when you
talk to them about God?" That same evening
Mother Teresa wrote in her diary: "I came home
this evening less tired than when I went out."

For some time now she had been trying to
ease suffering; and every tragic case left her with
a feeling of inadequacy. She would need
assistants, but "in order to endure this work for
long periods," said Mother Teresa, "greater strength
is needed, strength which only a religious life can
give." It was then that she outlined the regulations
for her future "Missionary Sisters of Charity". To
the usual three vows she added a fourth: the
freely-given and devoted service of the homeless.
"To serve the poorest of the poor of all classes
and creeds . . . to recognise God in the person of
the poor, the unwanted, the unloved: 'I was
hungry and you gave me to eat.' "

The Missionaries of Charity would recognise
that all the goods of this world — gifts of mind
and body, advantages of birth and education —

are the gifts of God, and that no one has the right
to an abundance of riches while others are dying
of hunger.

All she needed now were candidates.

Along came one of her former pupils, a pretty
Bengali girl from a good family. Her name was
Shubashini; she had a brown complexion, white
teeth, and wore a magnificent sari. "I want to
become one of your Sisters", she said.

"You are going to have to renounce everything,
even yourself," said Teresa. "Your life will have
to be one long self-denial. Think it over!" "I have
thought about it," replied Shubashini. Teresa
looked at her carefully. The qualities she was
looking for in her future missionaries were in the
first place health of mind and body, the ability
to learn, common sense, and above all a natural
gaiety and unfailing good humour. Shubashini had
all of these. "Come and see me again on Saint
Joseph's day."

The young girl came back on the appointed
day. She took off her beautiful sari and put on the
coarse garment, and took the name of Agnes which
had been Teresa's before she entered the convent.
Other young girls joined Sister Agnes. Soon there
were twelve of them, and the generous Mr Gomez
had to accept the transformation of his first floor
into a convent.

And so a new Congregation came into existence.
It was approved by Rome on the 7th October,
1950, as witness the decree of the Congregation
for the Propagation of the Faith. On 1st February,

1965, this religious Society became a Pontifical Congregation. Usually that takes a long time, sometimes thirty or forty years, but this favour so quickly obtained showed in a striking way the interest that Paul VI was taking in the admirable work of Mother Teresa.

In 1950, when Mother Teresa and her Sisters took their place in the Church, they carried out their work with a courage which had grown up without any foresight of the privileges which were to be theirs.

Then their life-pattern became established. They opened schools where, like everywhere else, life was regulated by the clock, prayers and classes. But more characteristic of the charitable activity of the new Society were the rounds of the shantytowns. Every morning the Sisters went into hovels which were the homes of the poorest of the poor. In Calcutta, if they had a long distance to travel they took the trams or the buses, which were about as comfortable as a salad basket — inside them they were cramped, jostled and almost suffocated. In Delhi there are no trams, and the hospital is twenty kilometres away. Any purchase outside the daily food therefore necessitates a long journey through dust-storms which make everything dance before the eyes, to the unbelievable din of motor-car horns in areas swarming with people.

There are men carrying buckets of milk, others on their way back from milking the buffalo. All along the pavement people doing their cooking on spits; vendors bawling out their wares and beggars repeating incessantly their monotonous chant. The Sisters have to fight their way through the widely represented animal kingdom also: hens, cocks, pigeons, cats, monkeys, crows, vultures; and cows rummaging in the dustbins.

One of the Sisters makes her way towards a square where there are thatched cabins. A door opens; at first she can see only absolute blackness — then as her eyes grow accustomed to this she can make out a long plank which takes up three-quarters of the room and serves as a bed. Dishevelled heads emerge from a pile of misshapen forms and there they are — six, seven, eight, — men, women, children and babies. They have all slept in their clothes, so to get ready all they have to do is splash some water on their faces, run a comb through their hair and brush their teeth with their fingers. There are no pumps, but some pipes come out flush with the floor, spilling out water which mixes immediately with the beaten earth.

On Sundays the Sisters go into the shantytowns at five in the morning to get the children up and bring them to church. To get to the church, the Sister usually goes along by a busy railway line walking between the tracks. When she hears the express coming, they all step off the tracks into a ditch full of water. The driver stops . . . and all the doors and windows open while the passengers look out at the children and the Sister standing waiting with their feet in the water! . . . But nobody is surprised, and nobody complains.

But the first priority of Mother Teresa's Sisters

are those who have only the hard pavement for a bed. At dawn thousands of people lying side by side on the ground, people who could easily be taken for corpses, wake up, cough, scratch themselves, and soil the ground. Others sleep on the stairways and entrances to houses, their ribs protruding. It is a battlefield of the outcasts of society: beggars, cripples and limbless people. In Pilkhana, separated from Calcutta by the famous Howrah Bridge which is crossed by 500,000 pedestrians every day, they sleep in a repulsive atmosphere generated by dampness, thousands of millions of buzzing flies, the smell of galleys and accumulated excrement, a sticky, blackish mud which has stagnated over kilometres of open cemented drains, encircling the dwellings. When the mud overflows, the people scrape up the top layer and make a pile of it on the street. A supposed refuse-collection service takes away this dirt from which the animals strive to eke out an existence.

This area of Howrah — once the rajah's elephant stables — today is the home of 4,000 people all living on top of one another.

The Home for the Dying

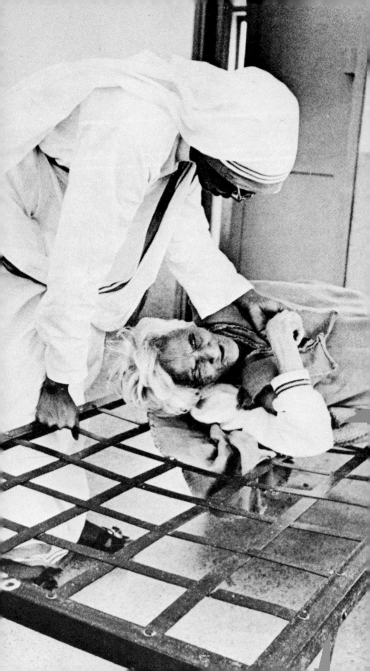

Mr Gomez's house was now too small for the
enormous numbers of sick people and Mother
Teresa went in search of somewhere else. The
papers had drawn public attention to the drama
of the people who were dying uncared for in the
streets, so Mother Teresa seized the opportunity
to say: "Give me a fairly central house in the
town and I will take care of the rest."

They gave her two rooms attached to the
Temple of Kalighat, dedicated to the goddess Kali.
The temple was built on the banks of a stream,
the Tolly, a much-frequented place of pilgrimage.
They came there from all over Bengal to see the
statue of Kali, the black goddess, covered with
so many offerings that you can see only her
golden tongue which stretches down to her chest,
as a sign of shame for having danced on corpses.
On the night of her feast the temple is daubed
with the blood of billy-goats, sheep and buffalo.
The butcher sticks the head of an animal on a
frame and slaughters it. Then the priest soaks his
finger in the warm blood and daubs the idol. How
different all this is from what is going on in the
annexes of the temple!

At first the presence of Christian nuns on their territory cast a shadow on the priests of Kali. Then one of them fell ill, and since the hospital was unable to admit him, Mother Teresa took him in and cared for him to the end. The other priests were overcome by this charity, so there were no further questions about the Sister in the blue-bordered sari. Furthermore, the corporation which had got her the two rooms now gave her a subsidy of £7,000.

This "Nirmal Hriday" ("Home for the Dying") was set up in 1954. Mother Teresa took in the most desperate cases: a poor helpless old lady who would have died in the gutter; a crippled young woman whom the hospital had refused to treat. A desperate, starving man who had thrown himself under a train and now had no legs. A boy with a broken leg, held together with two ounces of plaster of Paris and set all crooked.

"Because of the smell", one Missionary of Charity told us, "we had to carry outside a man with a gangrenous leg, swathed in rags. He developed a haemorrhage and the bones and muscles collapsed. A crow snatched up a bone which had fallen from his foot."

The nun went towards old men with skin more fragile than tissue-paper stretched over their chicken-like bones, who lay there silent and motionless, their eyes glazed; with a soothing hand she changed their dressings on foul-smelling sores. One day, the Sister told us, they brought Mother Teresa an old man who had been found in a ditch. He was a bundle of bones wrapped in a thin parchment of crumpled skin, but with a glimmer of life left in him. She washed him and cared for him, but the glimmer was too feeble. The old man muttered in Bengali: "All my life I have lived like a beast, and now I am dying like a human being. Why is this?" He started in wide-eyed amazement at the thin silhouette and the cross pinned on the whiteness of the sari. Then he died, taking with him his unanswered question.

Every morning ambulances and carts bring in the people found dying during the night on the pavements of Calcutta, people who have no one in the world, destitutes that no hospital would take in. Usually it is impossible to say whether they are dying of old age, of sheer exhaustion, or of loneliness. Young and old, they are all together. Some of them move slightly; others haven't even the strength to do that.

It sometimes happens, too, that the hospitals send out people who have families; then a son or a daughter will arrive in tears to know if their father or mother is in the house of the dying. Then there is the problem of names: the family gives one, the sick person another, and the ambulance-service yet another. Every admission is noted in a book, but for the people found in the street with no identity-card the ambulance-men give an approximate age — and that is how it happens that grandmothers of twenty years of age are admitted!

The first task for the Sisters is to wash the faces and bodies; dirt is so encrusted on these poor creatures that it has to be scraped off. The first few minutes are the most difficult because you have to get used to the smell, and if the Sisters were to forget for one moment that they are doing it for Christ, the task would become impossible. The new arrivals are disinfected from head to foot. When they arrive they are in a terrible state. They seem barely human. One never knows what one will find under the layer of filth covering an arm or a leg. Two hours before she died one woman was covered with ants.

There are also the sick people who are sent away by the hospitals: gangrenous, cancerous, with sores crawling with maggots. Those who are obliged to leave the hospital do so willingly, because they are frightened by it. For example, a Sister once talked to a woman who had all the symptoms of cholera. The sick woman answered all her questions affirmatively; but when the Sister mentioned the hospital, all the symptoms disappeared like magic. Fear of the hospital cured the poor woman who, to prove that she was better, got up, dressed and began a thankless sweeping job. The Sister did not insist, but simply asked one of the children to come and collect some medicines. It is not that the hospital staff have any lack of devotion, but simply that the hospital is overcrowded; no patient gets more than half a minute of attention; and they come for medical consultations in their hundreds. People die there every day without speaking, and the silence is broken only by the sudden shouts of two mad-women, or the tears of an old woman who thinks she has been forgotten in the food-rounds.

Here in the Home the people die with surprising tranquillity. There is perfect detachment; there is no bustle around the dying person, the anonymity is complete. In the room there are only soft whispers, feeble death-rattles mingling with the noise from the street, and with the discreet stirrings of the chef watching over a great pot of rice — the last meal of the dying. No tears, no cries, but respect for death which occurs every minute.

The bodies are given over to representatives of the religion to which the people belonged. The Hindus come and get them very promptly. Catholics and Protestants are slower. As for the Moslems, they often wait three or four days before taking the body from the morgue — which consists of a simple room with cement shelves.

"In the last few months," one of the Sisters told us, "I have seen four hundred men and women die. But our Nirmal Hriday is too small; and it is heart-breaking for us to have to put the less serious cases back on the streets. They go, sadly, without a word." At the house of the dying one sees the very limits of humanity, where holiness, revolt, resignation, despair and death are the framework of a strange universe. But also and above all there is love, a faithful love, to feel there is someone near him: the love of a Mother, of a Sister be she from California, from India, from the Balkans or from the Black Forest, who stays with him to the end.

Besides the "Home for the dying" there is the "Children's Home", as well as maternity homes, orphanages and schools. In Calcutta the children's home "Shishu Bhavan" is in fact an orphanage, for the children have been abandoned from birth. This institution takes in children from one day old.

The predominantly pink decoration reminds one of English nurseries. A picture of a very English rabbit stands beside a furry lamb. A child is playing with a teddy-bear on the floor. "We try to keep them happy here, but it is not the same as family life. One day I saw a young child who wasn't eating; his mother was dead. So I found a Sister who looked somewhat like his mother, and told her to devote herself entirely to the child; and his appetite returned."

All over the world there are children orphaned or abandoned through misfortune or shame. In India family pressures force unmarried mothers and young widows to desert their children, as a child would be an obstacle to marriage and there is no question of remaining single.

Because she is thinking of the future, Mother Teresa tries to have these children adopted, preferably in India, because it is necessary to foresee the complications of coloured children living with white people when they become adults. Thirty years ago one little girl was sent to America for adoption. She became a rich lady and came back to India to trace her family, and discovered that her father was a Moslem and her mother a Hindu. Why then should she be a Catholic? In India daughters are not appreciated — that is, unless they are remarkable for their fair complexion, beautiful face, and lively intelligence. Boys,

on the other hand, are always welcome. In
Shishu-Bhavan there are many premature children.
They thrive when put into packing-cases fitted
with a large bulb. The Sisters become very
attached to these little ones. One of them calls
a baby whose name is Christopher "my little
nephew".

The Sisters also have schools. In Calcutta there
are 4,000 children in their care. They give classes
in typing and sewing, set up joinery and metal
workshops; they start farming centres, cooperatives,
and all sorts of clubs; and yet remain, above all,
the servants of the poor. Mother Teresa was once
asked if she was not taking the risk of becoming
an institution, and her government an administration,
by diversifying in this way.

"I have often thought about this risk. We are
hoping to avoid it. And for this reason it is written
into our rules that all the Sisters — even the
Superiors — must serve the poor for at least a part
of *every* day."

City of Lepers, City of Peace

Saint Basil once said: "That coat you keep in your wardrobe belongs to a naked man; those shoes you allow to fall apart from disuse belong to a man who has no shoes; the money you are hoarding belongs to a poor man, the bread you have stored away to a hungry man." Is there anyone more naked, more deprived or more hungry than a leper who has to flee from society because of the fear and disgust of those better off than himself? That is why Mother Teresa looks on these unfortunates as an important responsibility.

The drama of leprosy and famine is heart-rending. It begins when a man states quite simply: "I am a leper." Then suddenly everything is closed to him; his wife leaves him; the unfortunate man is all alone. Mother Teresa goes through the desolate areas and seeks out the sick from their hiding places. "Why are you hiding yourselves away?" "I am ashamed and besides, people would throw stones at me." They hide their sores with leaves. One woman prostitutes herself at night to be able to eat. Another is blind and always alone. Yet another has gone mad, no doubt from despair, and insists on walking about on all fours; turning round and round in her hut. Another is rather like a beast at bay and when anyone comes to see her, she hides: "I thought it was the police." To be arrested for the crime of leprosy and thrown into the concentration camp of a leper colony is her nightmare. So she flees from the slightest noise.

In these slums the sisters are welcomed by a smiling leper with mutilated hands and toes; this cheerful man, looking very clean in his white "dhoti", acts as a nurse and is always with the nuns among the sick people. A Sister gives someone some clothes: how joyful that person looks! Then she stops for a long time to explain something to another.

One man is dying of pleurisy, and because his breath is stifled he groans loudly at regular intervals. Mother Teresa brings him a pillow, moves him a little and the death-rattle ceases. A woman holds her child to her with her painful stumps. She still preserves her sense of dignity, though living in a hut covered with old newspapers. So what can we say about all this? "Mother, I am an educated person. I was a clerk, I had a good job, I was earning 650 rupees a month. One day the neighbours complained: they said my face was unhealthy. The police came, what could I do? I had to leave. Only Mother Teresa could help me; she often tells us that leprosy is not a disgrace."

An old man is in a quandary: if someone looks after him, he will no longer be wretched and therefore will not be able to beg. That's another way of looking at it! For the lepers' slum is also a beggars' slum. They go out early in the morning and come back in the afternoon. In every area there is a "boss" who works out the times and places where they can beg. The Sisters and the police know well that no one can penetrate the slums except with the permission of the "bosses", whose authority is brutal. And at night it is better to pretend not to know what is going on in this gloomy courtyard.

Mother Teresa has seen lepers gone mad, and lepers in prison. And she is ashamed to eat heartily, to sleep without having nightmares, while thousands of people are rotting in abject misery. She has seen sores crawling with maggots and flies, infected rooms, empty pharmacies, frightened doctors, armed wardens, naked sick people, dazed people, crying out their despair and their hunger in a world of wretchedness, flies and filth.

The Sisters bring a little comfort to these unfortunates, give them injections, treat ulcers, look after them in various ways, improve the conditions they live in, give them medicines, and above all the comfort of friendship, while trying to free them from the medieval prejudices which exclude them.

"Touch a leper, touch him with love"

Mother Teresa's motto reigns over the eight colonies visited by the Sisters with their mobile clinic and the three dispensaries where more than fifty thousand sick people have been treated. Mother Teresa encourages them to provide for their own needs. Those who can use their hands make shoes out of old tyres, make cloth into bandages, cut out and sew their clothes, and do carpentry. At Christmas they have a midnight Mass. The evening begins with a play presented by the sick people, with dinner, cakes and music. Their gaiety, joy and gratitude are spontaneous and moving.

Fortunately the Missionaries of Charity are not the only ones fighting against sickness, for there are nearly three million lepers in India. In some places the percentage of sick people is as high as forty in the thousand. In Calcutta alone there are more than forty thousand lepers, and yet there is not a single hospital which specialises in the treatment of leprosy. There are, however, several organisations operating in India; the Hind Nivaram sangh, the Maharugi seva Mendal, the Ghandi Memorial Leprosy Foundation, the Ramakrishna Mission . . . . But Mother Teresa has directed her endeavours with an enthusiasm and a realism which have made them the most worthwhile, justifying St Francis de Sales' remark: "It only takes one good woman to overcome a city," or better still, to build one.

In fact what Mother Teresa and her nuns wanted was a permanent institution, and a big one, where as well as working to eradicate evil, they could make an effort to rehabilitate people who had been cured or were getting better, and where care, education and security, and above all, love and confidence, could help them to regain their dignity. That is why Mother Teresa was thinking of building a settlement at Asansol on a site given

to her by the government, and settling 400 leper
families there. She would call it the City of Peace,
and already she could visualise it growing up on
the huge empty site. There the lepers would have
workshops and gardens at their disposal, where
they could devote themselves to a trade or to
horticulture, be looked after and send their
children to open-air schools, where the pupils
would squat on the ground. A rehabilitation centre
on seventeen hectars of stone and glaze. All she
needed was the money, but she was not unduly
worried about that, knowing that God would
provide. Soon she saw coming alone the huge white
gleaming American convertible given to Paul VI
on his visit to Bombay. The Pope was giving this
sumptuous vehicle to her as a present and she
quickly converted it into money to build her leper-
town.

One allotment out of a projected fourteen was
erected immediately, a square red-and-grey
building. The main road of the City, to be called
Paul VI Avenue, was levelled along the bare land.
The future parks were planted. The ponds, where
ducks and geese would be raised, did not exist as
yet. Mother Teresa went on a tour of the site
with Sister Francis-Xavier: "Here we will have
trees, and along there hedges and garages; we will
have pools here; we have been given some little
fruit-trees, some mangos, pomegranates and apples.

"Over here we'll build a hospital and a school.
These forty small stools were made by the pupils
at Asansol . . . here a vegetable garden with
tomatoes, cabbages and peanunts . . " She dreams

about all this. Her hope for the future is based on everyday experience. God will not leave her by the wayside, for he knows that the lepers are Mother Teresa's children, and they know it too.

"While I was walking along with her," said Malcolm Muggeridge, "mixing with the crowd in the leper-town, I constantly heard people mumbling the word 'mother'. It wasn't that they had anything to say to her, but simply that they wanted to establish a link with her.

"From my own point of view I went through three phases when I was among the lepers. The first was horror mixed with pity, the second compassion pure and simple, and the third, reaching far beyond compassion, something I had never experienced before — an awareness that these dying and derelict men and women, these lepers with stumps instead of hands, these unwanted children, were not pitiable, repulsive or forlorn, but rather dear and delightful; as it might be, friends of long standing, brothers and sisters. How is it to be explained — the very heart and mystery of the Christian faith? To soothe those battered old heads, to grasp those poor stumps, to take in one's arms those children consigned to dustbins, because it is his head, as they are his stumps and his children, of whom he said that whosoever received one such child in his name received him."

There is only One Love

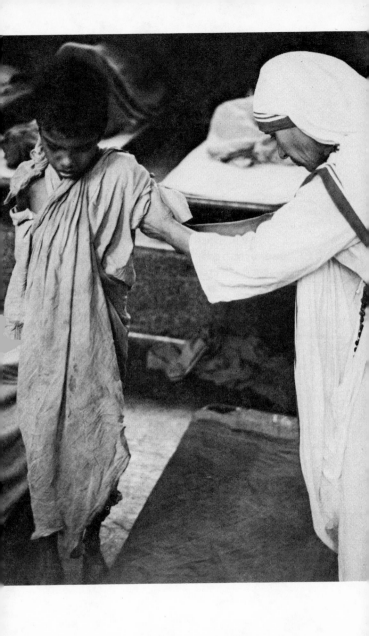

A starving beggar-woman was picked up off the
street, her body covered in sores, and while
Mother Teresa was washing her and putting her
to bed, she murmured: "Why are you doing this?"
Mother Teresa answered gently: "For the love of
God." For a long time back she had been making
Tertullian's words her own: "You have seen your
brother, you have seen your God." And who inspired
Tertullian to identify Christ with the little ones and
the wretched, if not Christ himself?

"I was hungry and you gave me to eat." . . . When,
Lord? "In truth I say to you, every time you did
it to one of these my smallest brothers, you did
it to me." The text of Saint Matthew, chapter 25,
is in everyone's mind. Mother Teresa, like Father de
Foucauld in the Sahara, Father Peyriguere in
Morocco, Martin Luther King among the black
Americans, and many others, has carried it out.
In her own way she develops it: "I was thirsty —
not for water, but for peace that satiates the
passionate thirst of passion for war . . . I was hungry
— not only for food, but for peace that comes from
a pure heart . . . I was naked — not for clothes,
but for that beautiful dignity of men and women

for their bodies . . . I was homeless — not for a
shelter made of bricks, but for a heart that understands, that covers, that loves.

"O beloved sick people, you are doubly dear to
me because you personify Christ, and it is indeed
a privilege for me to be able to care for you."
This is her very simple and very exacting theology:
"It is Christ we are touching in the slums, the
mutilated bodies, the children. And so we want
the poor to know that there are people who love
them, who *want* them.

"Let yourself be devoured by others," she often
reminds the Sisters. As for herself, she gives over
her whole being. She is a positive and steadfast
voluntary gift. Raoul Follereau said: "She is love
itself. I look on Mother Teresa as a heroine and a
saint: her face is taut and her eyes are dry. She
cannot afford to waste any of her strength on the
futile luxury of tears. She has no pity, in the
sentimental sense of the word. Pity is a pale sub-
stitute for love. She is love."

She also asks each nun destined to become a
worker in Christ's team in the slums to try to understand what God and society expect of her; to understand that Christ lives his life in her and through
her in the slums, so that the poor, when they see
her, should be drawn towards Christ and invite him
to enter into their homes and into their lives; that
the sick and those who suffer should find in her
comfort and consolation; that the children of the
streets should attach themselves to her, because
she reminds them of him, the Lord, the children's
friend.

In the logic of her charity, Mother Teresa considers that the individual is the only true value. Faced with the mass of starving and dying people, she does not see a crowd, but simply a starving or a dying person. Only one. "I never care for a crowd, only for one person. If I visualised a crowd I would never get started. The important thing is the individual. I believe in a person to person approach. Love is a fruit which is always in season. The greatest illness is not leprosy, but rather the feeling of not being accepted. The greatest scourge is indeed to forget the next person, above all when the next person is Christ himself."

Maybe it was in the light of this understanding of man and reality, which is Mother Teresa's inspiration, that Paul VI cried out: "Good does exist. Good is powerful. What comfort! What hope!"

Three words stand out above the crucifix in the chapel of the Missionaries of Charity: "I am thirsty." Mother Teresa has heard Christ's last prayer on the cross; with all her strength she has given herself the duty of answering it. But these words echo back to her from thousands of unfortunate people all over the world. That is why Raymond de Becker made the objection: "Whatever you do, will it not still be only one drop in an ocean of misery?" Mother Teresa answered: "India needs technicians, men of genius, economists, doctors and nurses for the future. She needs plans and coordinated action. But when will these plans come to fruition? We don't know. In the meantime people have to live. They must be fed, cared for and clothed. The ground

for our action is India today. For as long as present
conditions exist we need gifts, and charity holds
its own." At this reply Raymond de Becker left
Mother Teresa and went back to the areas of the
town where the anglicised Indians, snobbier than
their former masters, show only contempt and
indifference for the extreme wretchedness at the
feet of their extreme wealth.

"I glanced uneasily at the 'Indogothic' -style
Cathedral, the public buildings and the banks,
all in different architectural styles — Renaissance,
Corinthian, but never Indian. I passed the memorial
to Queen Victoria, of which a Bengali poet wrote:
' Will the city ever be able to forget the arrogant
person who built this "ice-cream" here!' I came
across rounded women, like those in a Rubens
painting, and greasy young men with watery eyes.
Among these skeletal people, grease signifies power.
Going back to the Great Eastern Hotel, where I
was staying, I thought back on my day. In the
huge dining room, the four or five gold-belted
waiters at each table busied themselves in fore-
seeing the guests' every whim. The jazz
orchestra on the stage was playing a popular tune
by Duke Ellington, 'St James Infirmary'. I ate a
meal which would have fed a family in the slums
for three days. And if I'd renounced it? The devil
whispered: 'It would serve no purpose.' What
troubled me most was the human mystery — not
the heroic faith of Mother Teresa and her spiritual
daughters, but that between their souls and the
souls of the most unfortunate of wretches there
was a correspondence, and a completion.

"Calcutta seems to me to be a high-spot for humanity, for it is impossible for anyone who is not deaf or blind not to recognise the most ravaging of human realities: in this abscess of the world it is impossible to avoid the pressing question of life. And the devil whispers: 'We must make more room in the world.' Yes, the simplest thing would be a bomb. And consenting to this solution would indeed be legitimate if it were not for the men and women who echo the cry of Golgotha: 'I am thirsty!' For humanity is justified as long as there exists, in the darkness of the third hour, some heretic Centurian who, in the face of the dying eternity of the world, deigns to pass the sponge soaked in vinegar to moisten the divine lips."

Derision? Sincere pity on the part of the Centurian? We don't know, but it is certainly with immense tenderness that the daughters of Mother Teresa carry on the work, and not only they but others also, whose hearts and hands have been opened. Good is contagious. "A great change is coming about now," says Mother Teresa. "The rich are coming to wash and feed the poor. They are doing a great deal of work. Before now we, as Christians, had never given them a chance. We thought that charity was for Christians only."

Mother Teresa paused to thank a Bengali woman who had accompanied her, and it was then that she made this amazing remark: "Oh no, Mother, it is I who must thank you; you have given me a chance to do something beautiful for God."

With the Missionaries
of Charity

To form an Indian community it is not enough
to dress in a sari, to pray with hands joined, to
share the meal of spiced rice. It is rather the
shared Rules, shared prayer and shared work with
a common aim which make for real unity.

A foreign Sister wrote: "After twenty-one
months sharing the life of the Indian Sisters I am
no more Indian than when I arrived; and I don't
consider that an obstacle. The Sisters are the
first to tell me that they feel completely 'at
home' with me, as indeed I do with them. So
we can fulfil and enrich ourselves together."

"Enrich ourselves" — let us think of this verb
in the light of the Sisters' absolute poverty. The
list of their possessions is very short: one enamel
plate and cutlery, two saris at 40p each, rough
underwear, a pair of sandals, a piece of soap in a
cigarette box, a metal bucket with a number on
it, a mattress and thin coverlet and a pair of
sheets. So, with her mattress rolled up under
her arm and everything else in her bucket, a
travelling Sister can carry all her possessions with
her.

When Mother Teresa founded her first house

in Venezuela, she arrived to find a 'fridge, a
washing-machine and comfortable furniture
which she gratefully returned to the donors.
Mother Teresa teaches the Sisters never to accept
remuneration for their work, but rather to
accept poverty in the spirit of joyful confidence.
Their life is a hard one: they rise at 5 a.m. and
work with the poor until 9 p.m., with only half
an hour's rest during the day. They have one day
of rest in the week, on Thursdays, which is
consecrated to adoration and reading. One Sunday
afternoon every month is set aside for correspondence and visits. The rules of the Missionaries of
Charity demand years of training, accompanied
all the way by hard labour in the service of the
poor. Firstly there is spiritual formation, then
practical and intellectual training in the duties of
nurses and doctors; some even study the law in
order to defend the weak. An austere existence
and discouraging work paradoxically strengthen
their joy of life.

"Our rigorous poverty is our safeguard," says
Mother Teresa. "We do not want to do what
other religious orders have done throughout
history, and begin by serving the poor only to
end up unconsciously serving the rich. In order
to understand and help those who have nothing,
we must live like them . . . The only difference
is that these people are poor by birth, and we are
poor by choice. It is nonetheless true that without
the conviction that it is Christ himself that we
see in the outcasts, such a life-style would be
impossible."

This faith in the presence of Christ is necessary when Mother Teresa gets discouraged, when she thinks of the fact that she is tackling a whole "ocean of misery" with one little spoon. She also retains her humility; while the whole world is talking about her, her feeling of insignificance and weakness stays with her. She works and prays in silence, because she says that "God and silence are friends, and the more we receive in silent prayer, the more we can give back in our active life."

Freed from the goods of this world, the Sisters are accustomed to moving around as Providence dictates. At the slightest sign, they are ready. One of them told us that "with a little organisation I could be ready to leave in half an hour." And she added: "I am staying in Calcutta; but I have not settled down there, and I have no intention of settling down anywhere. I prefer to be like a bohemian, going from place to place until I finally reach my eternal home."

The work may be hard, but the Sisters insist that it is very rewarding: "I will certainly not always be working here," said one of them, "and I am tempted to say 'What a pity!' But I go where Mother Teresa sends me; and anyway, it is always with the poor. We have nothing for ourselves. Always the same food. But I came because it is hard, and not out of romanticism or a taste for experience. I only want one thing: to devote myself entirely to the poor."

"It is with joy that we must contact Christ under his mask of wretchedness," says Mother

Teresa, "because joy is love. Joy is a prayer; joy is strength; joy is a net of love in which you can catch souls. God loves a person who gives joyfully, and the person who gives joyfully gives more. The best way of showing our gratitude to God and to other people is to accept everything joyfully. A joyous heart is the natural result of a heart burning with love. We wait patiently for Paradise where God is; but it is in our power to be in Paradise with him now; to be happy with him at this very moment. But to be happy with him now means:

"To love as he loves;

"to give as he gives;

"to help as he helps;

"to serve as he serves;

"to be happy with him now means to be twenty-four hours a day with him, hidden under his mask of wretchedness."

All those who help her, near and far, learn from her a very simple method of spreading love and joy. "It may be a simple smile, a short visit, just the fact of lighting a fire, writing a letter for a blind man, carrying in some buckets of coal, finding a pair of shoes, reading for someone; it is very little, indeed, but that would be our love of God in action.

"Even if we collect much less money this year, but if we spread the love of Christ further, if we give the hungry not only bread but love, our presence, human contact, 1971 could be the year of the real and living explosion of the love God brought to earth. Clothe the naked Christ out of charity and your regard for others. Shelter the homeless Christ, making your house a haven of peace, joy and love, by your attention to others, in your family and among your immediate neighbours."

The Sisters find joy in every situation; and the battle is won in advance, whatever they do. One day Mother Teresa arrived in one of her Communities at mealtime. She knows how hard are the tasks her daughters are subjected to: they must eat well. "From the next meal on," she decided, "you must all eat four 'chapatis' (little biscuits) instead of three." All the Sisters burst out laughing. "Why are you laughing?" asked Mother Teresa. "Up to now," explained one Sister, "with your permission, we have been eating three chapatis; but, wanting to be like the poor, we thought that two might be enough. Then we decided to make a novena to Saint Joseph to help us to decide: two chapatis or three? Then you came along and said, 'Four'."

Even when she is founding many centres and caring for the dying or expressing her deepest thoughts, Mother Teresa shines forth with a special light, that of one sent by God. Malcolm Muggeridge tells us: "Recently I was looking at the features of people who were listening to her — very ordinary people who were gathered together in a shed to hear her. All of them, young and old, plain and sophisticated, were radiant, hanging on her words; not for the words in themselves, for they were ordinary enough, but for herself. There

was a certain quality 'in' and 'on' the words
which held their attention. A luminosity seemed
to fill the school hall, lighting up the radiant
faces, penetrating their hearts and minds . . . When
the talk was over they all wanted to touch her
hand, to be in physical contact with her for a
moment, to participate in her life in some way.
She had the appearance of being so small and
fragile and tired from giving herself. However",
Malcolm Muggeridge continues, "it is in this way
that we arrive at salvation, in giving and not in
receiving; a society of giving, rather than of
consuming; to die in order to live. One old man,
not satisfied with holding her hand, lowered his
grey head and kissed her.

"Every day Mother Teresa meets Jesus: the
historic Jesus, which is really a contradiction in
terms: like a clock in eternity or a folding rule
without end. Jesus can only exist now, and, in
existing now, make the here-and-now last forever.
So, for Mother Teresa, the two commandments
' Love God and love your neighbour' become
reality together. In fact, they are inseparable. In
her life and in her work she gives examples of
what the relationship between the two is: that
if we don't love God, we cannot love our neighbour; and that if we don't love our neighbour,
we cannot love God."

The Foundation on the Five Continents

The Society of the Missionaries of Charity, founded on 7th October, 1950, at present comprises seven hundred nuns of different nationalities. The growth of the Society has been remarkable. Mother Teresa has integrated herself so deeply into the world of the unfortunates that any call, wherever it comes from, reminds her of her early calling: "I must do something." Guided by circumstances and intuition, she is gradually weaving an enormous chain which is linked up across the five continents.

It is in India, and more specifically in Calcutta, its birthplace, that the society is most widely spread: thirty of the forty houses are there. Their work is very varied: they have fifty centres in Calcutta specialising in medical and educational fields; a Family Planning Centre frequented by four hundred men and women; leper centres and thirty-two dispensaries in Delhi, Jhansi, Patna, Bhapalom and Amravati; schools in Calcutta, Agra and Kerala; a service for the old and dying in Calcutta, Goa and Bombay — all institutions whose clientele can be counted in the thousands.

Here are a few accounts and real examples.

The mission at Madurai is a very new one (1970).
Its first superior, Sister Anand, said: "We have
followed the footsteps of St John de Britto who
worked so hard for everyone here, and gave his
life for Christ. It is also the town of the cele-
brated sacred temple of the Hindus, who come here
on pilgrimages throughout the year. We work in
the shanty-towns and gather together abandoned
people from all over India." A hundred lepers —
hopeless cases, refugee beggars — are treated
regularly. Thanks to generous benefactors in
Malta, a large ambulance-service exists, which
allows five new centres to be served, and more
than five hundred mothers of families and
numerous children to be fed regularly. "We live
among them," says Mother Teresa, as she enters
the little colony built for the poor by the
Archbishop. Two blocks are reserved for poor
families: one room, a kitchen and a bathroom
at five rupees a month. The Sisters have their
convent there, and there are five apartments for
the most deprived. The third block houses the
dispensary and the men of the Nirmal Hriday
Home. The Sisters also visit the families, and with
the whole-hearted cooperation of the students
of "Fatima College" they organise adult classes
for the teaching of *tamoul,* a difficult language
which the Sisters have not yet mastered.

On one occasion when there was torrential
rain in west Bengal, a mile from Calcutta, Mother
Teresa and some of the Sisters used a boat on the
flood waters to save six hundred villagers stranded

on the roofs of their homes in Plonchonogram.

During the Indo-Pakistani conflict, Mother Teresa and her nuns took responsibility for a huge Bengali refugee camp. In their area more than 5,000 deaths were caused by a cholera epidemic. The Missionaries of Charity were untiringly dedicated and as soon as the war was over, Mother Teresa opened two houses in Bangla Desh, one of which was for the Bengalis, who suffered terribly.

In Ceylon, the Buddhist official with whom Mother Teresa had to deal told her: "I know and respect Christ, but I hate his Church. If you really do what you say, you can become a meeting place for us." And a year later: "I have watched you. Now I really believe that you are working for the poorest people. We are going to give you a lot of space in our monastery. You can have a dispensary there." However the government then changed its mind and refused visas. To the great distress of the people, the Sisters had to leave. But they have to be ready for things like that, too.

In Amman Mother Teresa founded a community to help the refugee camps after the six-day war. The Archbishop, Monsignor Pio Laghi, apostolic delegate in Palestine, and Monsignor Nolan crossed the lines from Jerusalem to Amman to welcome her, after the battle had ceased. Monsignor Nolan went with the Sisters to Djebal El Jaufa, the poorest area of the town.

During the crisis between the Jordanians and the Fedayins, the latter surrounded the Sisters'

house, ordering the nuns to line up against the
wall, and prepared to shoot them. At that moment
a Moslem came into the room and shouted: "Stop!
these nuns came to care for our poor people."
The Fedayins left, apologising.

The congregation was established in Venezuela
in Cocorote, not far from Caracas, in July 1965.
When the Missionaries of Charity came into the
church, all Cocorote resounded with the ringing
of bells, as if life had come back into this dead
country.

Sister Frederick writes: "Our Sisters are carrying out splendid work. Reverend Mother was
pleasantly surprised to hear them speaking fluent
Spanish. They prepare many adults for First
Communion, and give courses in dressmaking and
shorthand-typing. The distance between the
various camps is great, so the Sisters go around
by jeep. One of them has learned to drive, but
apprehensively, because in Venezuela you must
drive at colossal speeds — at least ninety kilometres
an hour!"

With the Archbishop's permission, the Sisters
became the "vicarias" (ministers); the curate of
the parish had died, so one of the nuns distri-
buted communion to the sick.

When Mother Teresa arrived in Tanzania, it was
said: "At last, here are Indians coming to Africa to
give rather than to *take!*" On 5th September,
1968, she opened a house at Tabora, with five
Indian sisters and the cooperation of Monsignor

Mihayo. The Sisters lived in old mud houses built at the turn of the century. Not knowing a word of the language (Kiswahili), they went on foot in search of the poor of Tabora, who, inside a week, called them "our sisters".

In Bourke Mother Teresa set up a station with the Australian aborigines who have been established on that continent for twelve thousand years. Like the American Indians, they were forced into "reserves" when the Europeans arrived, and it is difficult for an aborigine to find work and lodgings in the towns. Moreover, in spite of massacres by settlers — who once made out that these stone-age tribes were disappearing — they are constantly increasing in number. The foundation in Bourke, New South Australia, was opened in October, 1969, in the diocese of Broken Hill.

In Melbourne Mother Teresa began her Australian mission on 4th May, 1970. She brought love and support to many lonely and spiritually deprived lives — mostly old people. The Sisters visit these isolated people and do whatever needs doing for them, such as cooking and cleaning. As in many other regions, their best friends are the drunkards and alcoholics, who knock on their door at all hours, even after 11 p.m., asking for food and clothes. They show their gratitude and love by making gestures of respect and greeting when they meet them in the street; and if a visitor is having trouble finding the convent, they consider it a personal privilege to show them the way. The Sisters have started a hostel for the drunkards called "Hostel of Compassion"

One would have thought that the Third World would be a sufficiently vast challenge to Mother Teresa's charity, but Europe also has its slums and its thousands of homeless immigrants, so the Pope made Mother Teresa promise to open a foundation in the shanty-towns of the Italian capital. Mother Teresa had never even thought of it. To be a missionary in Rome!

That is how five Indian Sisters came to establish themselves in Rome, where, moreover, they couldn't even find a building. It was only after a great deal of difficulty that Mother Teresa finally found a hut at the foot of an old Roman wall, not far from the Appian Way. After that, helped by students, the Sisters built their own house, and showed themselves as first-rate bricklayers.

To start with, people were surprised by their being there. They must certainly have been dying of hunger in India! But people quickly understood that they were there to help others, not to ask for help themselves, and they had all the more respect for them.

Finally Cardinal Heenan opened a new centre in London on 8th December, 1970. It is the second noviciate of the Congregation. The centre is in a parish which has a large proportion of immigrants, maybe even a majority: many are Hindus, most of them Sikhs from Pundjab. Six months later a second centre was opened in a five-storey building in Saint Stephen's Garden.

It is not surprising that the community chose the top floor for itself, for the rest of the building houses the homeless.

Mother Teresa could not fail to be interested in the black Americans. A foundation was established for them in Harlem. "There are poor people everywhere; but here the real poverty is that no one wants them", Mother Teresa stressed on this occasion.

There is scarcely any question of drawing up a definitive list of the communities of the Missionaries of Charity. We are always one or two foundations behind: so, because she was in London when the civil strife in Northern Ireland was breaking out, Mother Teresa went to Belfast: "There is an act of love to be done there"; and she decided to set up a house.

Support for the Missionaries of Charity

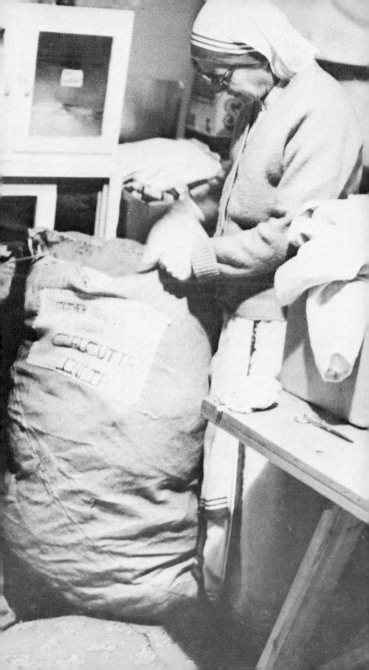

In a field of action getting wider all the time, it quickly became apparent that certain tasks were too great for feminine strength. Mother Teresa got young men interested in her work, entrusted them with the dying in the Home, and the boys in the schools, and with nine of them she founded the "Missionary Brothers of Charity". For three years she assumed responsibility for the young congregation which carried out extremely varied functions in the outlying areas of Calcutta. She was soon backed up by an Australian priest, Brother Andrew. When asked about the reasons for his choice, he answered simply: "The need is so evident."

On 25th March, 1963, Monsignor Souza blessed the beginnings of this new branch which has a house in Kidderpore. There are now eighty-six brothers, and one of them has been ordained since he entered the congregation. The brothers have experienced the many and deep joys of working with the suffering poor: the joy of seeing people relieved of a little of their misfortune, and the sick healed; fathers of families finding work; street urchins finding a home and responding like human beings who love and are loved; alcoholics and drug addicts overcoming their difficulties.

Brother Andrew tells us, "There was a man and his five-year-old son, near to death, cowering on a railway platform — the mother was already dead. We picked them up in a desperate state and brought them home. The father died a few days later without ever speaking. The boy stopped coughing, revived, and began to laugh and play with other little boys. Now he has found a home, food, and a little love."

The Brothers live on friendly terms with the Communists. "Most of the time," says Brother Andrew, "they come to us of their own accord, with their saddest cases. They send poor people to us with a little note asking us to help them. That is an opening for us. We are confident that they will realise that our only objective is human well-being, whether people belong to their organisation or not."

The rebound of Mother Teresa's work on the whole world is so great that people come forward to help everywhere, some as personnel, others as representatives of societies with other aims, while some, such as "the Friends of Mother Teresa" in France and Belgium, are specially organised for this purpose.

And so help arrives from all over the world in various forms: In *Australia,* it is a Christmas party given in the grounds of the Archbishop's house for the children of the poorest families.

In *Venezuela* Senora Sturno, who is in charge
of the co-workers, has taken to heart Mother
Teresa's desire to "do something beautiful for
God". A property belonging to her husband has
been given over with enthusiasm and love, ready
to welcome its first resident: this turned out to
be a man suffering from cancer.

In *Canada,* a group of bridge-players agreed to
give the proceeds of their game every week.

In the *United States* the ladies of the Deanery
Council of Catholic Women of Peoria have, for
eleven years, been giving their services to the six
clinics caring for mothers and children.

In *Brooklyn, New York,* the same organisation
sends money to the Foundation in Venezuela,
with large quantities of clothes, soap and other
gifts.

In *Tanzania,* the co-workers organise tombolas,
festivals and film-shows all the time.

In *Denmark* school-children regularly send
milk and vitamins to eight thousand children in
the Indian slums, and the "Pierre Khumsere"
Association has launched an operation called
"Milk Bottles S.O.S."

In *France,* since 1965, it is mostly the young
people who have taken an interest in the
Missionaries of Charity, as many conferences
have been given in schools on the new Congregation.
Hundreds of teenagers have sent postcards to
Mother Teresa telling her of their affection and
assuring her of their prayers. It was the young
people of France who were partly responsible
for the first foundation in Venezuela. Every year

young people and adults make great efforts to help Mother Teresa, putting several million old francs at her disposal for her work. Mother Teresa is also financed by "Secours Catholique", which is directed by Monsignor Rodhain.

In *Germany,* some parishes put an offerings box beside the crib and, after Christmas, send the money to Mother Teresa. Parcels and vitamin tablets are sent to Rome, Tabora and India. Old ladies knit blankets.

In *England* there is a lot of love and enthusiasm. Five ambulances have been blessed and sent to India; they have sent money for two thousand nine hundred and forty-five Christmas dinners. Every month tons of flour are sent to Calcutta, Bombay and Madras . . . Medicines and chilblain ointment have been given to the poor of Darjeeling.

In *Rome* students have built playgrounds and put in slides and swings.

In *Belgium* meetings of the Friends of Mother Teresa group take place regularly and discuss the main problems: the setting-up of European coordination groups, and above all, help for the lepers. M. Coppée has told the Royal family about it. Appeals have been made for medicines, materials, stamps, nylon stockings, plastic bags, pictures, post-cards. In this way large sums of money have been raised and forwarded. The dressmaking school started in Calcutta by Baroness Coppée and equipped by her with fifteen sewing-machines, deserves a special mention and indicates a good example to follow.

Apart from material aid, we must stress spiritual aid and goodwill in many forms, as when at the international day of prayer in the Anglican Cathedral at Guildford, the Reverend Ainger told more than a hundred different sects about Mother Teresa.

The International Association of Co-Workers of Mother Teresa was founded to unite all these different efforts and friendships; it is affiliated to the Missionaries of Charity and endowed with a constitution. The role of the associates is to support the Sisters and the Brothers in their mission of love among the poorest of the poor. They recognise that all the goods of this world are the free gifts of God, and that no one has a right to an abundance of wealth while others are dying of starvation (art. 8).

Sponsorship is a very effective means of cooperating in Mother Teresa's work: children are sponsored, put up as boarders in their own country, and given the possibility of pursuing their studies or their apprenticeship. The Sisters come to see them, and encourage those who know how to write to correspond with their adoptive parents. In this way they feel less alone in the world; and at the same time it is rewarding for the sponsors.

The money sent for a child is put into the bank. If a girl is not suited to study she is sent to a dressmaking school, and then she has a small dowry on her wedding day.

These sponsorships are by no means *adoptions*, as the Indian government is opposed to the idea

of young Indians leaving their country for good.
Many countries have approved this idea of
sponsorship:

In the *United States* children are sponsored,
six of them by the ladies of the "Deanery
Council of Catholic Illinois" in the Brooklyn area
of New York.

In *Malta* twenty-two children are sponsored.
Mother Teresa has moreover visited this island
for ten days and talked to hundreds of school-
children from various lay and religious organisations.

In *Belgium* a hundred and five children are
sponsored and benefit from regular contributions.

In *Austria* three hundred and twenty families
have applied to sponsor children.

In *France* almost eight hundred families are
sponsors.

In *England* more than five hundred families
have one or several sponsored children.

There is another kind of help which is above all
a silent and spiritual sharing: a section which
groups together all who by reason of illness,
infirmity or other handicap, are unable to help
actively. In their suffering, the members adopt a
Missionary Sister of Charity and so share the
labours and graces of her apostolate. Mother Teresa
describes what it means to "adopt a Sister". "You
who want to join the Missionaries of Charity as
spiritual and suffering members, will share in all
our prayers and all our work. The aim of our
Society is to appease the thirst of Jesus on the
cross for the love of souls by working for the

well-being of the poor. Who could do it better than you who are suffering? Your prayers and suffering are like the chalice into which we, who are working, can pour love for the souls we come across; therefore there is as much need for you as there is for us; together we can 'place all in him who gives us strength'. In order to heighten the sense of family, we should try to have the spirit of the Society in common. Now for a Missionary of Charity, it is necessary to give oneself completely to God, a sincere confidence, a perfect joy.

"Any suffering being who wishes to be a co-worker of the Missionaries of Charity is welcome; these are the true bearers of God's love, for I know that they will bring many souls to the feet of Jesus.

"So every Sister will have a 'second self', marked out by the emblem S.S.M.C., who prays and suffers for her; and each one will derive new strength from this support, and their lives will be like a burning light which will consume itself for souls." (Letter from Mother Teresa, 13th January, 1953).

Mother Teresa's achievements, which surpass all hope, are due to her conviction that nothing is impossible with God, and that the most way-out things in the eyes of the world are possible if God so wishes, since it is not herself acting, but God. So she abstracts her own will in order to let the Lord's will flow through her body and her words. It is simply that she has confidence in what she is doing and, as she said: "If I had not made the move of taking in a dying person from the street, there would have been no Missionary Sisters in Calcutta."

Behind the Scenes

Mother Teresa is thought of as a national heroine in India. The government grants her all kinds of privileges, such as visas and customs exemptions. The whole world talks about her; yet she retains all her humble freshness of soul amidst the reporters and photographers who buzz around her as soon as word gets out that she is in a place.

Yet she and her Sisters had to face up to extreme poverty and their faith was rewarded by visible proofs of God's love. Recently Mother Teresa and her daughters were looking for a house in London. A lady had a building which suited them perfectly; but she was very firm: "It costs six thousand five hundred pounds, to be paid immediately. I don't believe in anything, but I believe in your work." The Sisters set out around the town: visits, conferences, broadcasts; the donations flowed in. They counted up: there was exactly six thousand five hundred pounds!

The divine Providence has shown itself to Mother Teresa on many occasions, and makes her find exactly what she needs.

Sister Francis-Xavier telephoned her from Agra: she was urgently looking for fifty thousand rupees to start a children's home. "Impossible," Mother Teresa answered. "Where do you think we would find that much money?" A few minutes later the telephone rang. It was the editor of a newspaper: "Mother Teresa, the Philippine government has just awarded you the Magsaysay prize for all your work. A sum of money comes with it." "How much?" "Fifty thousand rupees." "In that case," said Mother Teresa, "I suppose God wants a children's home started in Agra."

A new postulant arrived, and there was no mattress for her to sleep on. Mother Teresa was about to open up her own mattress and cushion to take out enough stuffing to make an improvised mattress, when the door bell rang. It was an Englishman leaving Calcutta, and bringing his bedding to the Sisters. "He could have come beforehand or afterwards," said Mother Teresa. "He came at that exact moment."

There wasn't a grain of rice left. The novice in charge of the kitchen brought the empty box to Mother Teresa. At 4.30 p.m. an unknown lady arrived at the door of the convent with a bag: "Something made me bring you this", she told Mother Teresa. It was exactly enough rice for the evening meal, without an extra grain.

"We are coming to the end of our little store of mending cotton," said one of the Sisters. "We must get the Lord to take care of it." The Lord didn't wait to be reminded: the next morning a man brought Mother Teresa a parcel. How surprising, on opening the parcel, to find mending cotton instead of the usual clothes.

The Sisters had no more fuel for cooking. The last bits of wood, cardboard and paper had been burned and the cook was in despair, faced with a big pot of "curry" and the five hundred "chapatis" ready to go into the oven, knowing that a ravenous community would soon be home. One of the kitchen assistants was given the job of putting the matter in the Lord's hands in the chapel: "Lord, you said that you would give to those who asked; please, we have no more wood." She had just left the chapel when the halldoor bell rang and wood arrived.

A very delicate proof of the attention of Providence was given on the feast of the Immaculate Conception: high Mass was to be sung by Monsignor Barber. It was the prelate's mother's birthday, and the Monsignor's parents were to attend the Mass. Mother Teresa was worried, knowing that there was only one prie-Dieu and that the parents, being old, would have difficulty in kneeling on the floor like the Sisters. He who worries about the least of the sparrows looks after our most humble needs. A few hours before the ceremony a prie-Dieu with red cushions arrived; and that evening Mother Teresa said to the Sisters: "I wonder who sent it?" With one voice they all said: "Jesus!"

However, our Lord has not always granted Mother Teresa's prayers, or rather he has granted them in his own way.

It had rained incessantly for five days: ninety-five boxes of powdered milk were going to be lost.

They had been put in the yard of the Children's Home. "What are you doing, Lord?" cried Mother Teresa. "The milk is outside." At the end of the fourth day she had made all sorts of complaints to the Lord. Even her crucifix, which she had hung in the rain among the boxes, had changed nothing. Nevertheless, her confidence unshakable, she knew that all would be well. In the surrounding villages the rain fell for twelve days, making the little houses of more than a hundred people uninhabitable. On the fifth day the sky cleared in Calcutta, and Mother Teresa hurried to see what had happened. The boxes were floating in water, but the milk was perfectly dry. There was one box with a damaged lid: Mother Teresa, to test the depth of God's love, said to our Lady when she was opening it: "What happened to this one?" only to discover that not a single drop of water had penetrated the broken wood. And Mother Teresa cried out: "What earthly husband would have done that for his beloved!"

The following act is a touching homage rendered as much to God as to the instrument he used.

A man with cancer had sores so nauseating that Mother Teresa had put him into the room with the dead people. While she was caring for him, he flooded her with abuse: "How can you put up with my stench?" he shouted. "Swear that it gives you pleasure to see me in this state!" "That is nothing compared to what you are suffering," she answered. After a minute he calmed down: "What sort of people are you, in

this house? I have never seen anyone act like you."
Later he propped himself up on his elbow with
an undefinable expression on his face: "Glory to
you!" he murmured. "No," Mother Teresa answered,
"Glory to you, because you are suffering with
Christ!" This simple answer shows, by antithesis,
what sufferings are when separated from Christ.
"They crystallise, as nothing else can, the dilemmas
and nightmares of life without God." Malcolm
Muggeridge said of suffering: "It is an inflamed
nerve which, touched, gives rise to howls of rage
and anguish, especially today. Simone de Beauvoir,
watching her mother die in agony of cancer, saw it
as 'an unjustifiable violation'; as something 'as
violent and unforeseen as an engine stopping
in the middle of the sky'. The image is significant.
When machines jam and go wrong, we hate them
utterly and look around for a manufacturer
or mechanic to curse. In the eyes of those who
see men as machines, God is that manufacturer,
and the mechanic his priest."

Mother Teresa sees things quite differently.
For her, suffering and death are not the simple
breakdown of a machine. Her sights are higher:
suffering and death are essential parts of our
human adventure. They are an integral part of
the plan of God who made us, not unchangeable
entities of this small world, but future inheritors
of an "other" heritage. Such is the price of life!
Suffering belongs to God; so that the experience
of every life says: "Your will be done." "To say
it standing before the cross which, itself, stands
for God's suffering in the person of a man, and

the redemption of man in the person of God:
'Your will be done.' This is what Mother Teresa
is saying in such a simple way in every one of
her smiles and gestures."

On 6th January, 1971, Mother Teresa
received a cheque for fifteen million lire from the
John XXIII Peace Prize, from the hands of Pope
Paul VI. She thus became the first woman in the
world to get the Oscar of Charity, in the great hall
of the Consistorium full of cardinals, members of
the Corps Diplomatique in formal dress, Mother
Teresa's family and some of the Sisters of her
Congregation.

Cardinal Villot revealed that the jury, when
making its decision, was inspired by the Peace
Day motto: "Every man is my brother."

Madame Paronetta Valier explained that Mother
Teresa's work had seemed to the Pope to be
worthy of being proposed for the attention of a
world ravaged by so much hate and cruelty. The
Pope commented on the seeming paradox:
certainly Christ taught that good must be done
in silence, but he also said that the light should
not be put under a bushel. "This prize has been
presented so that good may spread and be fertile;
hoping that this good will serve as an example, it
is presented to our eyes and those of the public.

"Evil is contagious, but so is good. And good
is often done by means which are out of proportion to the task in hand. Sometimes this dispropor-
tion only becomes greater as the work progresses.

Then the work acquires a value which is greater than the merit of its concrete action.

"The work becomes a testimony which indicates to public opinion the existence of a problem needing a solution. In silence it teaches not only the necessity but also the possibility of resolving it." And Paul VI concluded:

"Once again in the history of the Church and in society in progress, the Gospel has been accomplished and again the joy of good is lighted, the hope of an ideal life, the luminous truth of the words of Irenaeus: 'The Glory of God is man fully alive'.

"All this takes on great importance in the modern world which is growing up in the effort at sincerity and understands the enormous needs which have appeared in present-day society on a world-wide scale: ignorance, hunger, sickness, crumbling standards, and the dangers of its own conquests. Man must now make enormous efforts for his fellow man; efforts that powerful and generous undertakings have put in motion; but a need which is called for by these very undertakings is that the human ideal should not grow dim, but that it should always have numerous and new witnesses . . . She who presents herself as a Missionary of Charity is an apostle of the brother-hood. That is why we are giving her the Prize for Peace . . ."

Monsignor Benelli, deputy to the Secretariat of State, has explained the meaning of this gesture:

"In this society which is becoming more and more aware of economic inequalities, and has

come to see the problem of peace simply as the
elimination of these inequalities, Paul VI wanted
to show that justice must be the basis for peace,
but that it must be accompanied by charity.
Justice alone is not enough. He wanted to remind
this society, which believes in the power of money
as an instrument for the promotion of progress,
of another element, namely poverty, as an
instrument for development consisting of detachment and sacrifice. In a world where the law of
capacity, of returns, is becoming more and more
preponderous, he has awarded the prize to a
Sister who is devoting herself to the most useless
human beings on the production line, to those who
can give nothing in return to our consumer
society.

"It is not only important to do something
about development, but also to think about the
way in which we do it. Mother Teresa's work is
based on total impartiality, sincerity and auth-
enticity. That is what the needy want . . . If
planning is necessary, we must not wait until the
planners are ready to make a move. Life and
death will not wait for our plans. Love is never
planned . . . '"

This prize made it possible to go ahead with
the "Shanti dan" leprosy foundation at Raigahr,
which is called the City of Peace. U Thant, when
he was secretary general of the United Nations,
said: "I consider this recognition to be worthy
of the Holy Father's great predecessor, whose
bigness of heart and goodness were acknowledged
by all."

This great honour has caused all eyes to turn towards the light that Mother Teresa spreads, like a lamp of love, in our world of shadows. The amazing thing is that as a frail woman and a foreigner with no resources, she started out with her own two hands, and a faith which moved mountains and touched the heart of India, to lighten the weight of wretchedness which bears down on the masses of outcasts. Then people came to her aid; she gathered together young men and women and brought a new Congregation into being, whose shining love for suffering humanity reflects that of Christ himself. She travelled all over the world to start a crusade of good will.

A gospel lived out, we were saying at the beginning: by spreading the Good News, surely Mother Teresa has made us hear how deaf and see how blind we really are? But neither she herself nor those she has taken to work with her will ever suppress poverty: "There will always be poor people among you," said Christ; but he declared himself a solid ally of the poor and the suffering in general. Many of us had forgotten that.

The more this sad century is rent by scars, the more we can base our hopes on the testimony of this extraordinary woman who comforts the nakedness or pain of some and invites others to share in the joy of giving.